THE ANCESTOR ALBUM

Tony McCarthy was born in Cork City and educated at the Model School, Coláiste Chríost Rí and University College Cork. He lives in Cork, with his wife Angela (*née* Healy) and their children, where he teaches English and History at Christian Brothers' College. Author of *The Irish Roots Guide*, he now edits the quarterly family history magazine *Irish Roots*.

For Steve, Paul, Johnny and Mary Claire

THE ANCESTOR ALBUM

Tony McCarthy

THE LILLIPUT PRESS

First published in 1994 by
THE LILLIPUT PRESS LTD
4 Rosemount Terrace, Arbour Hill,
Dublin 7, Ireland.

Cover design by Jarlath Hayes
Set in 12 on 14 Cochin
Printed in Dublin
by ßetaprint

CONTENTS

PART ONE

Fill-in Charts

THE JOB IS URGENT

Since you've started reading this book, there is no need to tell you that doing your family tree is important. What you may not realize, though, is that it is also urgent. The best sources of family information are old people. You're never likely to come across a bunch of documents that could compete with a bunch of grand-aunts. We never know how long old people will be with us. That is why the job is urgent.

The Ancestor Album tells you what to ask the older members of your family. The book also provides fill-in charts to record and arrange the information you collect. When you are finished, you should have an impressive, five-generation family tree. You should also have enough information to allow you to advance much further if you decide to make a hobby of family history.

NOTE

Before you start filling in the spaces in the following pages, you should first decide what generations you are going to use. If you are an adult with children, you might prefer to put the name of one of your children as the first generation and put yourself and your partner as the second generation.

Remember also that you have four grandparents: two from your father's side and two from your mother's. To avoid confusing them, it is usual to call your father's parents your *paternal* grandparents and your mother's parents your *maternal* grandparents. (from the Latin: *pater*, father; *mater*, mother)

The simplest of all family tree charts is a two-line diagram. Line one shows the parents, the child is on the second line. I give my own as an example.

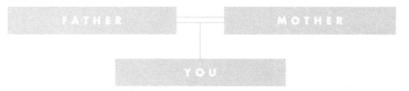

Fill in your details in the boxes provided below.

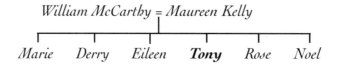

If you wish, you can add more details, the names of your brothers and sisters for example, or the date of your parents' marriage, your date or place of birth. Fill in the more detailed chart below.

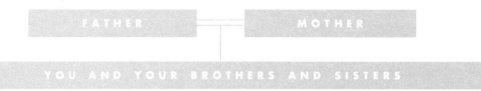

ADD A THIRD GENERATION

Do a similar chart, this time putting your father in as the child and your father's parents (your paternal grandparents) as the parents.

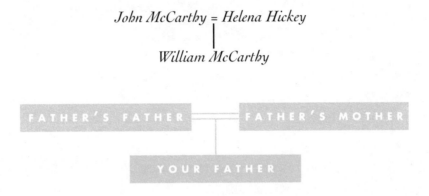

John McCarthy = *Helena Hickey*

William McCarthy

FATHER'S FATHER — **FATHER'S MOTHER**

YOUR FATHER

Now do the same for your mother's side of the family. Fill in your mother's name as the child and your mother's parents (your maternal grandparents) as the parents.

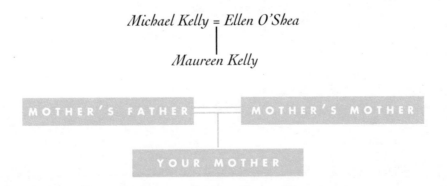

Michael Kelly = *Ellen O'Shea*

Maureen Kelly

MOTHER'S FATHER — **MOTHER'S MOTHER**

YOUR MOTHER

MORE DETAIL

Now add more detail to your father's family tree. Write down the names of his brothers and sisters, that is your uncles and aunts. If possible, list them in the order in which they were born.

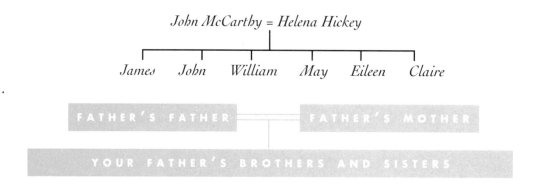

John McCarthy = Helena Hickey

James   John   William   May   Eileen   Claire

FATHER'S FATHER — FATHER'S MOTHER

YOUR FATHER'S BROTHERS AND SISTERS

Do the same for your mother's side of the family.

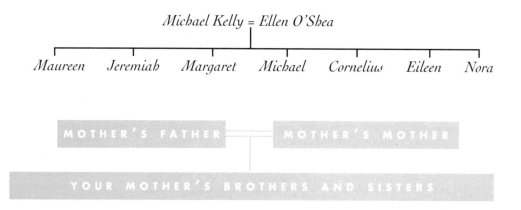

Michael Kelly = Ellen O'Shea

Maureen   Jeremiah   Margaret   Michael   Cornelius   Eileen   Nora

MOTHER'S FATHER — MOTHER'S MOTHER

YOUR MOTHER'S BROTHERS AND SISTERS

4

GETTING HELP

Up to this point you should have required little or no help. This is because most people can name their four grandparents from memory. To make more progress, it is likely that you will have to get help from your parents. Just like everybody else, they should be able to name their grandparents. Their grand-parents are your great-grandparents. You can add a whole new generation on to your family tree just by asking.

But perhaps one or both of your parents are dead, or maybe they just don't know the names of their grandparents. No need to despair. Just ask their brothers or sisters — your aunts and uncles. You made a list of them on the previous page. Remember, your uncles and aunts from your father's side had the same grandparents as your father; your mother's brothers and sisters shared the same grandparents as your mother. Your uncles and aunts are as likely as your parents to be able to name your great-grandparents.

You may have to call or write to people you haven't contacted for years to get infor-mation about your great-grandparents. Getting in touch with relatives you barely know can be a bit embarrassing. Just remember, the day will come when there will be nobody to contact. Gathering family information is an urgent business.

ASKING THE RIGHT QUESTIONS

Apart from their names, there are other facts about your great-grandparents that you should try to find out. The most important of these items are:

DATE OF BIRTH

A good guess will do.

PLACE OF BIRTH

Try to get as exact an address as possible for place of birth. The name of a county is too vague. Try to discover the name of the town or village. If the great-grandparent was born in the country get the name of the townland; the name of the street if born in a city.

DATE OF DEATH

Again, a good guess will do here. This date will probably be more accurate than the date of birth since your parents, aunts or uncles may remember the actual death.

These bits of information could be very useful if ever you decide to trace your roots further back into the past.

RECORDING YOUR INFORMATION

Many of the dates you write down will be based on guesswork. Some people are good at guessing. They may be old, have good memories and be interested in what you are doing. Other people may not be so good. You should always write down who gave you the information. That makes it easier to judge how seriously to take it.

'*Circa*' is the Latin word for 'about'. It is often used before dates to show that they are guesses rather than fully correct. Sometimes '*c.*' is used for short. 'Born' is often shortened to 'b.', and 'died' to 'd.'

The following example puts these suggestions to work. My Aunt Eileen told me that her father's mother was called Johanna Nelan and that she died around 1895. I recorded the information like this:

MY FATHER'S GRANDPARENTS

His mother's mother

Name: *Johanna Nelan*

Place of birth: *Causeway, County Kerry*

Date of birth: c.*1843*

Date of death: c.*1895*

Information given by: *Aunt Eileen*

YOUR GREAT-GRANDPARENTS 1

You know the questions to ask and where to get the answers. When you have gathered the information, fill in the spaces on this page for your father's side of the family, and on the next page for your mother's side of the family.

MY FATHER'S GRANDPARENTS

His father's father

Name:

Place of birth:

Date of birth:

Date of death:

Information given by:

His mother's father

Name:

Place of birth:

Date of birth:

Date of death:

Information given by:

His father's mother

Name:

Place of birth:

Date of birth:

Date of death:

Information given by:

His mother's mother

Name:

Place of birth:

Date of birth:

Date of death:

Information given by:

YOUR GREAT-GRANDPARENTS 2

MY MOTHER'S GRANDPARENTS

Her father's father

Name:

Place of birth:

Date of birth:

Date of death:

Information given by:

Her mother's father

Name:

Place of birth:

Date of birth:

Date of death:

Information given by:

Her father's mother

Name:

Place of birth:

Date of birth:

Date of death:

Information given by:

Her mother's mother

Name:

Place of birth:

Date of birth:

Date of death:

Information given by:

TAKING STOCK

W e have now dealt with four generations — you and the three generations before you. You will notice that the number of people in each generation doubles as you go back. There is one of you. You have two parents, four grandparents and eight great-grandparents. So far we have dealt with fifteen people in your family tree. The diagram below makes this clear.

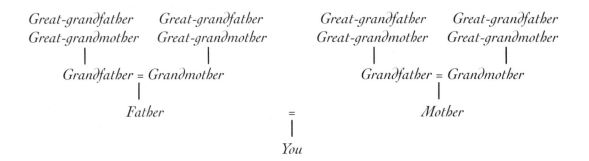

When we come to deal with the fifth generation you will have another sixteen ancestors to cope with. That's the number of great, great-grandparents we all have. Before tackling the next generation, it would be a good idea to draw up a family tree using the four generations we already know about.

If you did not manage to get all eight great-grandparents, it does not matter. Fill in the names of the people you managed to locate and leave the other spaces blank. After a few generations, blanks begin to appear in all family trees.

FAMILY TREE OF FOUR GENERATIONS

Below is a diagram of my family tree for four generations. The lower half of the page is laid out with green boxes for you to fill in your family.

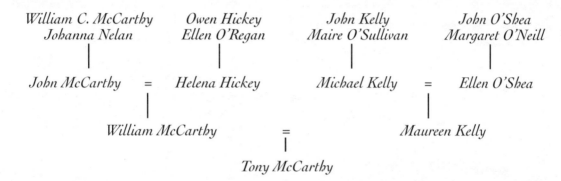

YOUR FATHER'S GRANDPARENTS

HIS FATHER'S FATHER	HIS MOTHER'S FATHER
HIS FATHER'S MOTHER	HIS MOTHER'S MOTHER

YOUR MOTHER'S GRANDPARENTS

HER FATHER'S FATHER	HER MOTHER'S FATHER
HER FATHER'S MOTHER	HER MOTHER'S MOTHER

YOUR GRANDPARENTS

YOUR FATHER'S FATHER	YOUR FATHER'S MOTHER	YOUR MOTHER'S FATHER	YOUR MOTHER'S MOTHER

YOUR PARENTS

FATHER	MOTHER

YOU

THE FAMILY CIRCLE

There is another way of arranging your ancestors' names. The diagram should make detailed explanations unnecessary. Your own name goes in the centre, the names of your mother and father are written in the next segment. The third section is for your four grandparents and the outer part is divided into eight spaces for the names of your eight great-grandparents. Study the diagram before writing your family names into the family circle chart on the next page.

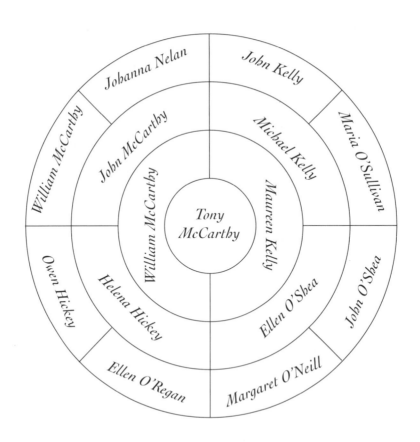

YOUR FAMILY CIRCLE

Now fill in the chart below with the names in your four generation family tree. Practice your curved writing first or else fill in the spaces lightly in pencil. Do a neat job. You are making an important historical document for your family.

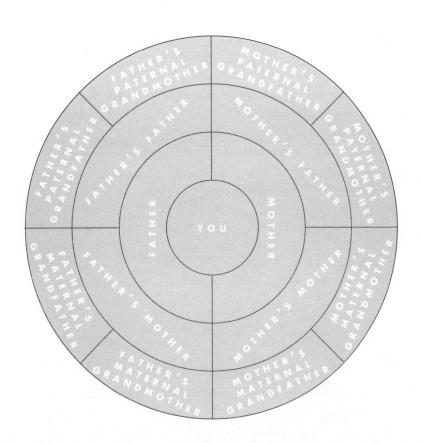

Now we come to the hard part, finding the names of the members of the fifth generation — your great, great-grandparents. Let's review the situation. We decided to get all the information for our family tree simply by asking people. There is no point in asking your father, mother, aunts or uncles about your great, great-grandparents. Their memories are unlikely to be able to stretch back farther than their grandparents. Their grandparents are your great-grandparents and you should have got those names already.

Who, then, is likely to know the names of your great, great-grandparents? The answer to that question is this: their grandchildren.

The grandchildren of your great, great-grandparents are your grandparents, your grandaunts and your granduncles.

So your grandparents, your grandaunts and your granduncles can tell you the names of the people in the fifth generation.

5 Great, great-grandparents	———————▶	This generation are
4 Great grandparent		the grandparents of
3 Grandparents	◀———————▶	this generation.
2 Parents		So generation number
1 You		3 should be able to give
		the names of generation
		number 5.

MAKING A LIST

The problem at this stage is this: there may not be many of the people you need to question left alive. The first thing to do is to make a list of your grandparents and their brothers and sisters. Your parents should be able to help you draw up this list. Your grandparents' brothers and sisters are your parents' uncles and aunts.

THE LISTS

A   *Your father's father and his brothers and sisters:*

B   *Your father's mother and her brothers and sisters:*

C   *Your mother's father and her brothers and sisters:*

D   *Your mother's mother and her brothers and sisters:*

<u>Underline</u> those who are still alive.

WERE YOU LUCKY?

If you have even one name underlined on the previous page, you could get the names of up to four of your great, great-grandparents. Then your family tree chart will be five generations long.

If you are lucky enough to have one name in each of the four lists underlined, you have a good chance of getting the names of all sixteen of your great, great grandparents.

If you have nobody underlined on the lists that you drew up on the previous page, you will get no further with your family tree now. Turn to the end of this section and use the information you have already collected to fill in the charts. If you want to go further with your family history, the second part of this book will advise you on what to do next.

ASKING MORE QUESTIONS

You must now call or write to the people you underlined on the lists. You must ask them for the names of their four grandparents, places of birth, dates of birth and dates of death. Write down the information each person gives in the spaces below. Write the name of the person who gave you the information also.

INFORMATION TO BE COLLECTED FROM SOMEONE ON LIST A, PAGE 15
(The numbers will help you write the names in the correct parts at the end of this section.)

paternal grandfather 1

Name:

Place of birth:

Date of birth:

Date of death:

Information given by:

paternal grandfather 3

Name:

Place of birth:

Date of birth:

Date of death:

Information given by:

paternal grandmother 2

Name:

Place of birth:

Date of birth:

Date of death:

Information given by:

paternal grandmother 4

Name:

Place of birth:

Date of birth:

Date of death:

Information given by:

paternal grandfather 5

Name:

Place of birth:

Date of birth:

Date of death:

Information given by:

paternal grandfather 7

Name:

Place of birth:

Date of birth:

Date of death:

Information given by:

paternal grandmother 6

Name:

Place of birth:

Date of birth:

Date of death:

Information given by:

paternal grandmother 8

Name:

Place of birth:

Date of birth:

Date of death:

Information given by:

paternal grandfather 9

Name:

Place of birth:

Date of birth:

Date of death:

Information given by:

paternal grandfather 11

Name:

Place of birth:

Date of birth:

Date of death:

Information given by:

paternal grandmother 10

Name:

Place of birth:

Date of birth:

Date of death:

Information given by:

paternal grandmother 12

Name:

Place of birth:

Date of birth:

Date of death:

Information given by:

paternal grandfather 13

Name:

Place of birth:

Date of birth:

Date of death:

Information given by:

paternal grandfather 15

Name:

Place of birth:

Date of birth:

Date of death:

Information given by:

paternal grandmother 14

Name:

Place of birth:

Date of birth:

Date of death:

Information given by:

paternal grandmother 16

Name:

Place of birth:

Date of birth:

Date of death:

Information given by:

NEARLY THERE

You have an enormous amount of important work done now. You have gathered up information that will certainly not be available so easily in the future. You have created a family history that generations of your family will value and preserve.

Only one thing remains to be done. That is to fill in the charts in the following pages. Do this work in your neatest handwriting. Up to now you have been recording facts, so the presentation was not so important. The three charts that follow are the parts of the book that people will want to look at.

The first chart allows you to record all the basic information you collected about your grandparents, great-grandparents and great, great-grandparents. If you or some other member of your family decide to take up family history as a hobby and start doing research in documents, this chart will be of great use.

The second chart is the family circle chart. It has room for you, your parents, grandparents, great-grandparents and great, great-grandparents — thirty-one people in all.

The third chart tells who collected this family history. You must write down your name and other details. This may not seem important now, but future generations of your family would like to know who saved their family history for them. Don't be modest. Fill that in too.

1

Name

Place of Birth

Date of Birth

Date of Death

3

Name

Place of Birth

Date of Birth

Date of Death

5

Name

Place of Birth

Date of Birth

Date of Death

7

Name

Place of Birth

Date of Birth

Date of Death

2

Name

Place of Birth

Date of Birth

Date of Death

4

Name

Place of Birth

Date of Birth

Date of Death

6

Name

Place of Birth

Date of Birth

Date of Death

8

Name

Place of Birth

Date of Birth

Date of Death

Name

Place of Birth

Date of Birth

Date of Death

Name

Place of Birth

Date of Birth

Date of Death

Name

Place of Birth

Date of Birth

Date of Death

Name

Place of Birth

Date of Birth

Date of Death

YOUR PATERNAL GRANDFATHER

YOUR PATERNAL GRANDMOTHER

YOUR FATHER

Name	11 Name	13 Name	15 Name
Place of Birth	Place of Birth	Place of Birth	Place of Birth
Date of Birth	Date of Birth	Date of Birth	Date of Birth
Date of Death	Date of Death	Date of Death	Date of Death

0 Name	12 Name	14 Name	16 Name
Place of Birth	Place of Birth	Place of Birth	Place of Birth
Date of Birth	Date of Birth	Date of Birth	Date of Birth
Date of Death	Date of Death	Date of Death	Date of Death

Name	Name	Name	Name
Place of Birth	Place of Birth	Place of Birth	Place of Birth
Date of Birth	Date of Birth	Date of Birth	Date of Birth
Date of Death	Date of Death	Date of Death	Date of Death

YOUR MATERNAL GRANDFATHER   YOUR MATERNAL GRANDMOTHER

YOUR MOTHER

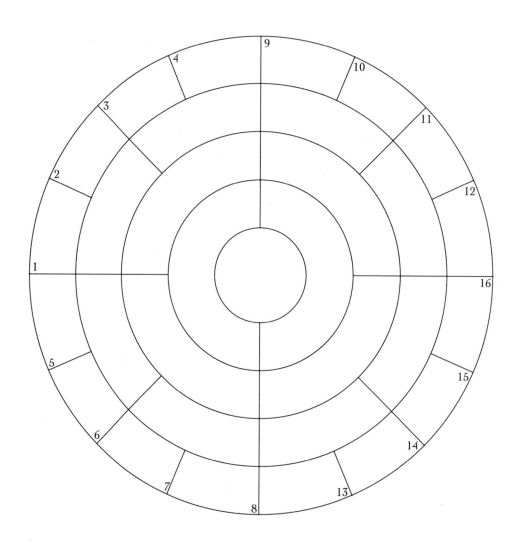

This is to certify that

I

of

wrote this Family History.
It is based on my own memory
and the memories of relations
whom I questioned.
I have carried out the work
carefully and I believe that
it is correct.

Signed:
Date:

PART TWO

Proceeding Further

THE SHADES

If you filled in Part One of this book, you should be able to name many of your ancestors now. Perhaps you have seen old photographs of some of them and could even recognize their faces. Imagine all of them lined up in rows. Behind your parents are your four grandparents. In the next row, your eight great-grandparents. A new generation comes into being about every thirty years. So, away there in the distance, ten generations back, are your great, great, great, great, great, great, great-grandparents, who lived three hundred years ago. There are more behind them stretching back further into history, ancestors beyond counting.

In parts of Africa, people believe that their dead ancestors are all around them, taking a strong interest in what they, the living, are doing. These spirits are called 'The Shades'. It is dangerous to get on the wrong side of those shadowy characters. They have the power to ruin your life.

If your ancestors could come out of the shadows, what would they say to you? Imagine the great multitudes of ghosts from the past, pushing and jostling to get close. What would they whisper in your ear? How can we know that unless we learn more about them?

THE FIRST PEOPLE

Ireland was one of the last parts of Europe to be occupied by man. Human communities have lived in Africa for two million years and in Europe for about 700,000 years. Though man reached southern England 400,000 years ago, the earliest signs of human activity in Ireland are less than 10,000 years old.

The earliest settlers probably came from Scotland. Because of the thick forests that covered the country, they settled near rivers and lakes and travelled in small boats made of animal skins. These Stone Age people spent all their time just trying to survive: hunting, fishing and gathering wild fruits and berries. They made almost no mark on their environment, so we know very little about them.

A more advanced Stone Age people came to Ireland around 6000 years ago. They were farmers. They cleared the forests to make fields for planting their crops. Because more food was produced, the population increased from about 3000 to about 100,000. Not everybody had to be involved in food production, so some people could now do other types of work. Spectacular megalithic (*mega* means great, *lithos* means stone) tombs were built, like Newgrange in the Boyne valley.

Bronze and gold were introduced to Ireland about 4500 ago. The National Museum in Dublin has the greatest collection of prehistoric gold objects in Western Europe.

THE CELTS

Five hundred years before the birth of Christ, the Celts invaded Ireland. They were a people from continental Europe. One Roman writer described them as 'war mad'. They fought from chariots and collected the heads of their enemies. The Celts had iron weapons and they conquered the earlier Irish settlers who still used bronze.

Celtic families lived in fortified farmhouses called ring-forts. The ruins of about 40,000 ring-forts can still be seen in Ireland, spread throughout almost every one of the 32 counties. The Celts also built huge hill-forts like Tara, Navan Fort, and Dún Aonghusa. In later history, the Celts became known as the Gaels or the Irish.

When St Patrick arrived in Ireland in AD 432, the population had reached 500,000. The people lived in about 150 small kingdoms.

The Irish became enthusiastic Christians and the period from the sixth to the ninth century is often known as the Golden Age. During this time famous illuminated manuscripts, like the Book of Kells, were produced; beautiful gold objects such as chalices were made, monasteries were built and genealogies and histories were written down. Irish monks became missionaries and took Christianity back to parts of Europe where it had been wiped out by invasions of barbarians.

THE VIKINGS

By the early ninth century monasteries had become very wealthy, especially in gold and silver objects. The prospect of easy loot attracted Scandinavian raiders known as Vikings. The Irish had been softened by hundreds of years of freedom from foreign invasion and were not able to resist very well. Using their longships in rivers and lakes, the Vikings penetrated deep into the country terrifying and destroying Irish communities. At first, the Vikings made hit-and-run raids. Later they established permanent settlements. The cities of Dublin, Cork, Limerick, Waterford and Wexford all began in this way. These were the first towns to be built in Ireland. The Vikings eventually became Christians and began to intermarry with the Irish. When Brian Boru defeated them at the Battle of Clontarf in 1014 they were not expelled from Ireland. They continued to control small coastal towns.

SOME SURNAMES TRACEABLE TO THE VIKINGS

Betagh	*Cotter*	*Coppinger*	*Dowdall*
Dromgoole	*Gould*	*Harold*	*Palmer*
Plunkett	*Skiddy*	*Sweetman*	*Trant*

SURNAMES

Up to the time of Brian Boru, most people in Ireland did not have surnames. They had personal names which were not passed down from one generation to the next. Some people believe that Brian Boru, as High King of Ireland, ordered the use of second or family names. Whether this is true or not, many people started using surnames during his reign in the tenth and eleventh centuries. Surnames did not come into general use in Britain, France and other European countries until the thirteenth and fourteenth centuries, so Irish surnames are among the earliest in Europe.

The Irish took their surnames from various sources. Most used the personal name of their father or that of a famous ancestor. They put 'Mac', meaning 'son of', in front of their father's name. McDermott, for example means son of Dermot. 'O' meaning 'descendant of' was used in front of a famous ancestor's name. O'Toole means the descendant of Tuathal.

Some surnames came from occupations: McGowan, for example comes from 'mac an gabha', son of the blacksmith; McIntrye comes from 'mac an tsaoir', son of the workman. Personal qualities and place-names were also used as surnames. Brody comes from the Irish 'bródach' meaning proud; Athy and Galway are examples of surnames derived from place-names.

The Normans took over England in 1066 when William the Conqueror defeated the Saxons under King Harold. A little over a hundred years later, they came to Ireland. From a military point of view, they were vastly superior to the Irish. They wore armour, which the Irish considered cowardly. They fought from horseback which was another big advantage. Their archers could pick off Irish soldiers whose sword and battleaxes were useful only at close quarters. When they captured an area, they built castles in order to hold on to it. The ruins of some of these fortified castles can still be seen. The Normans took over the Viking towns and some Irish kingdoms but they did not manage to conquer the whole country. In time, the Irish began to copy the Norman way of fighting and the Normans began to copy the Irish way of life. For centuries, the kings of England took little interest in Ireland.

By 1500 there were about fifty small, independent kingdoms in Ireland, some ruled by Irish chiefs and some by descendants of the Norman lords — who were now known as the Old English.

NORMAN NAMES

Barry	Bellew	Bermingham	Burke
Carew	Clare	Cogan	Dalton
Darcy	DeCourcy	Delamere	Dillon
Fitzeustace	Fitzgerald	Fitzhenry	Fitzmaurice
Fitzsimons	Fitzstephen	Gernon	Grace
Hussey	Keating	Lacy	LePoer
Marshall	Montmorency	Mortimer	Nangle
Nugent	Petit	Prendergast	Purcell
Roche	Staunton	Taaffe	Talbot
Tuite	Tyrell	Verdon	Vesey

THE ENGLISH

In the sixteenth century all these little kingdoms were conquered by England. The people who carried out this new conquest are known as the New English. They regarded the Irish and the Old English as their enemies. When they conquered an area, they brought in 'planters'. These were English people who were willing to come over to Ireland and settle down. In this way, it was hoped to bring the English way of life to Ireland.

The Irish and the Old English resisted for about a hundred years. Eventually they were defeated. Ulster held out the longest. Hugh O'Neill, the last great Irish chief, had his kingdom there. Hugh and his Spanish allies were defeated in the battle of Kinsale and in 1607 he and over a hundred of his followers fled from Ireland. This event is known as the Flight of the Earls. All his land was taken over and planted, particularly by Scots Presbyterians.

ENGLISH NAMES

Adams	Andrews	Arnold	Ashe	Atkinson
Baker	Barr	Barton	Bates	Bennett
Berry	Bingham	Bolton	Bradshaw	Brooks
Canning	Carlisle	Carter	Christy	Cooper
Cox	Crowe	Downes	Edwards	English
Field	Fisher	Freeman	Goodwin	Hall
Harper	Harris	Harrison	Hawthorne	Henry
Hewitt	Hill	Holmes	Hopkins	Hunter
Jackson	Jenkins	Johnson	Johnston	Kidd
Lamb	Little	Long	Mitchell	Morton
Nash	Osborne	Pearson	Richardson	Roberts
Robinson	Salmon	Shaw	Short	Simpson
Small	Somers	Swan	Taylor	Thornton
Turner	Walker	Wall	Waters	Watson
Webb	Webster	West	White	Woods

The Scots changed Ulster from the most Gaelic part of Ireland to the most British. They cleared the woods and forests, changed the open pasture land into small, well-tilled fields and built over twenty new towns. By 1640 there were over 40,000 Scots Presbyterians living in Ulster. The total population of Ireland was about two million.

In 1641 a major rebellion broke out in Ireland. The Irish and the Old English combined against the New English planters. The war was fought over religion and land. With the help of Oliver Cromwell and his army the planters won. More land was confiscated from the Old English and the Irish, both of whom were Catholics, and more planters were brought in to occupy it.

Wars continued to be fought over land and religion. The Irish Catholics always lost and most of them became tenant farmers renting land from Protestant landlords.

In the twentieth century, some of the old enmity between rival groups still exists, especially in Northern Ireland.

SCOTTISH NAMES

Campbell	Cameron	Fraser	Gordon
Graham	Kerr	McGregor	McIntosh
McKay	McKenzie	Miller	Morrison
Paterson	Ross	Sinclair	Stewart

REFUGEES

Ireland was not the only country where religious wars were fought. In 1685 Louis XIV banished all Protestants from France. These French Protestants were known as Huguenots and over 10,000 of them came to Ireland. They were welcomed because Ireland was controlled by Protestants. Most of them were skilled and educated and made an important contribution to Ireland.

HUGUENOT NAMES *Barré, Blacquiere, Boileau, Chaigneau, Du Bedat, Champion, Chenevix, Corcellis, Crommelin, Delacherois, Drelincourt, Dubourdieu, Du Cros, Fleury, Gaussen, Logier, Guerin, Hazard, La Touche, Le Fevre, Lefroy, Lefanu, Maturin, Perrin, Saurin, Trench, Vignolles.*

The Palatines were another persecuted religious minority. They were from Germany. Over 800 families came to Ireland in 1709. They were settled on farms in Limerick, Kerry and Tipperary. The descendants of the Palatines were still speaking German in the nineteenth century.

PALATINE NAMES *Baker, Bovanizer, Bowen, Doube, Delmege, Gilliard, Latchford, Ligier, Millar, Lodwig, Modlar, Pyper, Reynard, Ruttle, Shire, Stark, Switzer, Tesky.*

Over the last six hundred years, Jews came and went out of Ireland. At the end of the last century the present Jewish community, which numbers about 3000, came to Ireland from the Baltic states and Eastern Europe. They were fleeing from persecution at the hands of the Tsar.

JEWISH NAMES *Begin, Coplan, Fridberg, Greenberg, Hasselberg, Maisell, Matufsky, Rabinovitch, Rossin, Statzumsky, Stuppel, Wachman, Wedeclefsky, Weiner, Winstock.*

In the twentieth century other groups have come to Ireland in small numbers: Italians, Indians, Chinese and, in recent years, Vietnamese, Rumanians and Bosnians.

What kind of surnames are in your family tree? Are they Gaelic, Viking, Norman, Welsh, English or Scottish? It is likely that you have a mixture of several different types. Surnames can help you to find out when your ancestors first came to Ireland and what countries they originated in. In the case of Gaelic names in particular, they can help tell you what counties your ancestors are likely to have inhabited in the past.

It is important to remember, though, that this is only guess-work. Many Vikings and Normans adopted Irish surnames even to the extent of using 'Mac' and 'O'. In 1465 a law was passed requiring Irish people who lived in areas controlled by the English to take English surnames. The names suggested were: colours, such as white, black, brown; names of towns, such as Cork and Kinsale; names of trades such as smith, carpenter, cook.

Some people 'translated' their names into English taking totally different surnames. Lehane often became Lyons; Ó Sionnach became Fox.

Edward MacLysaght wrote several books on Irish surnames. They are available in most libraries. Unless your surname is very unusual, you will find a short history of it in one of his books: *Irish Families: Their Names Arms and Origins* (Allen Figgis and Co. Ltd: Dublin 1957); *More Irish Families* (Irish Academic Press: Dublin 1982).

HOW COMMON IS YOUR SURNAME?

A hundred years ago Robert E. Matheson listed, in order, the hundred most common surnames in Ireland. He worked out how common a surname was by counting the number of births for each surname in the year 1890. He figured that the more babies bearing a particular surname, the more common the surname. There were 1386 Murphy babies born in 1890, which was by far the greatest number for any surname, so Murphy topped the list. Here are the rest of them:

1	Murphy	26	Wilson	51	Sweeney	76	Kenny
2	Kelly	27	Dunne	52	Hayes	77	Sheehan
3	Sullivan	28	Brennan	53	Kavanagh	78	Ward
4	Walsh	29	Burke	54	Power	79	Whelan
5	Smith	30	Collins	55	McGrath	80	Lyons
6	O'Brien	31	Campbell	56	Moran	81	Reid
7	Byrne	32	Clarke	57	Brady	82	Graham
8	Ryan	33	Johnston	58	Stewart	83	Higgins
9	Connor	34	Hughes	59	Casey	84	Cullen
10	O'Neill	35	Farrell	60	Foley	85	Keane
11	Reilly	36	Fitzgerald	61	Fitzpatrick	86	King
12	Doyle	37	Brown	62	Leary	87	Maher
13	McCarthy	38	Martin	63	McDonnell	88	McKenna
14	Gallagher	39	Maguire	64	McMahon	89	Bell
15	Doherty	40	Nolan	65	Donnelly	90	Scott
16	Kennedy	41	Flynn	66	Regan	91	Hogan
17	Lynch	42	Thompson	67	Donovan	92	Keeffe
18	Murray	43	Callaghan	68	Burns	93	Magee
19	Quinn	44	O'Donnell	69	Flanagan	94	McNamara
20	Moore	45	Duffy	70	Mullan	95	McDonald
21	McLaughlin	46	Mahony	71	Barry	96	McDermott
22	Carroll	47	Boyle	72	Kane	97	Moloney
23	Connolly	48	Healy	73	Robinson	98	Rourke
24	Daly	49	Shea	74	Cunningham	99	Buckley
25	Connell	50	White	75	Griffin	100	Dwyer

EMIGRATION

Sean Murphy is a professional genealogist. He wanted to find out if Matheson's list is accurate for the 1990s. He calculated how common a surname is today by counting the number of telephone subscribers per surname. He found that the top ten names are still the same, but they are now in a different order.

Here is Murphy's top ten 1990 with Matheson's top ten 1890 beside it.

	1890		1990
1	Murphy	1	Murphy
2	(O')Kelly	2	(O')Kelly
3	(O')Connor	3	(O')Sullivan
4	(O')Sullivan	4	Walsh(e)
5	Walsh(e)	5	Smith
	Smythe		
6	(O')Brien	6	(O')Brien
7	Ryan	7	(O')Byrne
8	(O')Byrne	8	Ryan
9	Smith	9	(O')Connor
	Smythe		
10	(O')Neill	10	(O')Neill

When Mary Robinson was made President of Ireland in 1990 she said: 'There are over seventy million people living on this globe who claim Irish descent.' She was not exaggerating. Between 1801 and 1921 at least eight million people emigrated from Ireland. Emigration has continued at a high rate ever since. The children, grandchildren and great-grandchildren of emigrants easily make up President Robinson's seventy million.

The descendants of Irish emigrants consider themselves to be American, Australian, Canadian and various other nationalities as far as loyalty to a state is concerned. But being Irish is still very important to most of them. Their values and outlook on life have been shaped by their Irish ancestry. People of Irish descent are noted for their strong interest in education, their regard for family life and their warm feelings towards Ireland.

St Patrick's Day is now celebrated in almost every country in the world with the wearing of the shamrock and big parades. No other national festival has become so international.

THE HOBBY OF FAMILY HISTORY

Family history is one of the most popular hobbies in the world. People take it up for different reasons. A kind of self-interest is the main reason — everyone is interested in himself/herself and our ancestors are really a part of us. They made us what we are. By finding out about our ancestors we find out more about ourselves.

The seventy million Irish who live abroad are always keen to find their roots. They know that at some point their ancestors made a decision to emigrate, to leave family, friends, relations and a familiar neighbourhood for a better way of life. The old home across the sea is a mystery and a fascination for their descendants. Americans, Australians and Canadians often go to a lot of trouble and expense to trace the old homestead back in Ireland and to visit it. Many an emigrant's grandchild found this to be one of the highlights of his/her life.

Tracing ancestors is like detective work. That aspect attracts some people to the hobby. They love travelling to libraries and record offices, reading old musty documents, finding clues that lead on to other discoveries. They are not satisfied until they have found out everything.

PROFESSIONAL GENEALOGISTS

A professional genealogist is someone who will trace your roots for you for a fee. You can write to a professional genealogist describing what you already know about your ancestors and what else you would like to find out. A professional has experience of searching all kinds of Irish records. He or she is able to judge whether or not a search for information is likely to be a success. Having assessed the situation, he or she writes back to the client giving an opinion and explaining how much a search would cost. There are about twenty-five professional genealogists in Ireland. Some of them are members of an organization called the Association of Professional Genealogists in Ireland (APGI). You can write to them at the Genealogical Office, 2 Kildare Street, Dublin. Many of the genealogists from Northern Ireland are in an organization called the Association of Ulster Genealogists and Record Agents. Their address: Glen Cottage, Glenmachan Road, Belfast BT4 2NP, Northern Ireland.

COURSES IN FAMILY HISTORY

Sean Murphy, a Dublin-based professional genealogist, runs a number of night courses in family history at University College Dublin. The introductory classes total ten hours over as many weeks and are intended to start people on the path to tracing their ancestors. For those who wish to undertake more intensive study, a longer course is available. It totals forty hours spread over twenty weeks. It includes visits to some record offices. Subjects like the origin and development of surnames, Gaelic genealogies, septs and heraldry are covered. A certificate is awarded at the end of the longer course.

More information concerning these courses can be obtained from the Adult Education Office, UCD, Belfield, Dublin 4; telephone 01 7061416.

YOU CAN DO-IT-YOURSELF

If you decide to take up family history as a hobby, you will need to learn about Irish records — the documents in which you might expect to find information about your ancestors. About twenty guide books have been written to help you, most of them in the last ten years. Some of them are out of print, others are not much good. The following four books are the best guides and they are all available in libraries and bookshops.

An Introduction to Irish Research by Bill Davis (£4)

Irish Genealogy: A Record Finder, edited by Donal Begley (£8)

The Irish Roots Guide by Tony McCarthy (£4)

Tracing Your Irish Ancestors by John Grenham (£10)

Bill Davis's book is the easiest of the four and is for the complete beginner. The *Record Finder* is meant for people who know the basics and who want to progress onto more difficult record collections. There is something for people at all levels in the other two books.

A 36-page, glossy magazine called *Irish Roots* is published every three months. It provides information and advice on all aspects of constructing family trees and keeps its readers in touch with what is going on in the world of family history. If you can't get it in the shops, you can order it from Belgrave Publications, Belgrave Avenue, Cork. It costs £8 for a one-year subscription.

There are two bookshops in Ireland that specialize in family history. One in Dublin and one in Belfast: The Heraldic Artists, 3 Nassau Street, Dublin 2; Familia, 64 Wellington Place, Belfast.

THE IRISH GENEALOGICAL PROJECT

The IGP aims to computerize all records that are useful for family history, and to set up a family history research centre in every county in Ireland. There is a centre in most counties now but no county has all of its records fully computerized yet.

At these centres you are not personally allowed to use the records. You make an enquiry by calling in or writing and an employee of the centre consults the records and gives you a report. There is a charge for the service. It varies from £30 to £100, depending on the amount of work your inquiry involves.

The names and addresses of the county-based centres are available from: Bord Fáilte, Baggot Street Bridge, Dublin 2.

ARCHIVES

You can get information on your family tree from two main sources: asking people and searching through documents. When your relations have told you everything they know, you can make more progress only by means of documents. These documents are stored in various public offices, mainly in Dublin. The General Register Office and the National Archives are two of the most important.

Since 1864, all births, deaths and marriages in Ireland have to be registered. Details of them have to be written into special books called registers. Copies of the registers are kept in the General Register Office in Dublin. If any of your ancestors was born, married or died in Ireland anytime after 1864, his/her name and other details will be in one of the register books. It is not surprising that this office attracts many people who are interested in tracing their roots.

In the 1860s a Public Record Office was built in Dublin. Records such as wills, old taxation and census forms, land records and court records were stored there. Anybody who wished could go in and examine the records free of charge. The documents stored in the Public Record Office would be very useful now for tracing ancestors. Unfortunately, during the Civil War in Ireland, the building where they were stored was blown up and most of the records destroyed. Since then, other, similar records have been collected. They are stored in the National Archives in Bishop Street, Dublin. Family tree researchers use them a lot.

MORMONS

Joseph Smith founded a new religious group in New York in 1830. It became known as the Mormons or the Church of Jesus Christ of Latter-day Saints. One of the beliefs of the Church is that ancestors may become members. Some details about the ancestors have to be found before this can happen. This is why the Mormons are interested in family history.

They founded the Family History Library in 1894 in Salt Lake City, Utah, USA. Its purpose is to collect copies of documents that can help people trace their roots. It is now the biggest library of its kind in the world.

Most of its records are on one and a half million reels of microfilm. Two hundred microfilm camera operators travel around the world filming important records. Every year about 50,000 reels of microfilm are added to the collection.

All the records are stored in the Wasatch Mountains south-east of Salt Lake City. They are held behind nuclear bomb-proof steel doors in six storage rooms under 700 feet of granite.

Copies of the records can be looked at in the Family History Library. The Mormons also run 1500 family history centres in fifty-five countries where their records may be used. There are three of these centres in Ireland, one each in Dublin, Belfast and Cork. People who are not Mormons may use the records. The members of the Mormon Church are not allowed to try to convert people who are using their records.

TOURISM

Tourism is a very important industry. Many people are directly or indirectly employed in it. Bord Fáilte has the job of bringing tourists into the Republic. The Northern Ireland Tourist Board has the more difficult job of getting tourists to come to Northern Ireland.

Golf, fishing, beautiful scenery, a relaxed pace of life, friendly people — these are some of the things highlighted by the tourist boards to try to attract people to Ireland.

In 1988 it was discovered that 36 per cent of visitors from North America gave tracing their Irish ancestry as one of the main reasons why they came to Ireland. The two tourists boards then got more involved in promoting family history as an Irish attraction.

The two boards now produce leaflets, posters and brochures on family history. You can get information on clan rallies, genealogy courses, and heritage centres free of charge from them.

ADDRESSES

Bord Fáilte, Baggot Street Bridge, Dublin 2.
Northern Ireland Tourist Board, 59 North Street, Belfast BT1 1ND & on Nassau St, Dublin 2.

GENEALOGICAL RESEARCH DIRECTORY

Family history research can take a very long time to complete. If you have to travel to record offices or employ a professional genealogist it can also be very expensive. There is always the chance, especially when you have managed to go back several generations, that a distant relative whom you have never heard of is doing exactly the same work. He or she could be researching the same family and have very useful clues that could help you to make progress. The question is, how do you find out?

The answer is: by using research directories. Various directories are published each year which list families that are being researched. By far the biggest of these is the Genealogical Research Directory (GRD), published every year since 1981 by the Library of Australian History.

The GRD lists in alphabetical order family names that are being researched. Obviously, there are many different families with the same surname, so a time period and a place is given with each entry. The name and address of the person doing the research is also given, so it is easy to get in touch with anyone whose research interests you.

It costs £14.25 to put up to 15 entries in the GRD. For that you also get a free copy of the book which has over 1000 pages and over 100,000 entries.

SOCIETIES

Family history is a very popular hobby in Australia, Britain, Canada and the USA. In those countries people like to get together to discuss their pastime. There are almost one hundred family history societies in Britain and several hundred in the USA. Members meet each month to listen to lectures, swap ideas and generally to help each other find out more about their ancestors.

The biggest Irish society is the Irish Family History Society. It has around 600 members, most of whom live abroad. The 130 or so who live in Ireland are scattered throughout the country. They do not meet except at their annual conference.

Ireland has a few local family history societies. The Republic has four: two in Dublin, one in Wexford and one in Cork. Northern Ireland is served by The North of Ireland Family History Society which has seven branches: one each in Belfast, Bangor, Ballymena, Killyleagh, Larne, Lisburn and Omagh.

Anyone can start up a local family history society. Just contact one of the existing societies for advice.

ADDRESSES

North of Ireland Family History Society, c/o Department of Education, Queen's University of Belfast, 69 University Street, Belfast, Northern Ireland.
The Irish Family History Society, P.O. Box 36, Naas, County Kildare.
Wexford Family History Society, 24 Parklands, County Wexford.
Dún Laoghaire Genealogical Society, 14 Rochestown Park, Dún Laoghaire, County Dublin.
Cork Genealogical Society, c/o Cork County Library, Farranlea Road, Cork.

CLANS

An Irish Clan Gathering usually involves people of the same surname getting together at a place that has some historical connection with their surname. Normally the programme of events includes a visit to a castle, a talk on the history of the surname, the election of an honorary clan chief, and a banquet at which there is an opportunity to talk to other 'members of the clan'.

The popularity of Clan Gatherings in the early 1990s is due to the efforts of Rory O'Connor. In 1987 he said in a speech to a gathering of the O'Connor clan that he would set it as his purpose to organize all the clans in Ireland.

He was as good as his word. He spent all his free time at the job. He managed to get help from many quarters, including the governments and tourist boards of Northern Ireland and the Republic.

By 1989 twelve clans had been organized and a Clans of Ireland Office was opened in Dublin in November of that year. The high point for the clans movement came in 1992. The Clans of Ireland Office had registered 165 clans by then and it was thought that Clan Rallies would attract tourists to Ireland. Half a million pounds, from the International Fund for Ireland, was spent on promoting an Irish Home-coming Festival. Fifty clan gatherings were advertised to take place during the festival month of September. The rallies failed to bring in big numbers of people from abroad. This was a serious setback to the clans movement.

The Clans of Ireland Office is still open: 2/3 Kildare Street, Dublin.

REGISTERED CLANS

The following Clans are registered in the Clans Office, Dublin:

Allen	Devlin	Keating	McGettigan	O'Connor	O'Shea
Ahern	Duffy	Kelly	McGillycuddy	O'Dea	O'Sullivan
Baker	Dunne	Kennedy	McKenna	O'Dochartaig	O'Toole
Barry	Elliot	Kenny	McLoughlin	O'Donnell	Patterson
Burke	Evans	Keohane	McManus	O'Donoghue	Pierce
Bradshaw	Ferris	Kiely	McNally	O'Dowd	Power
Brennan	Fitzgerald	Kilkenny	McNamara	O'Driscoll	Quinlan
Buckley	Fitzgibbon	Killoran	McQuillan	O'Dwyer	Quinn
Butler	Gallahue	Kinnane	McSweeney	O'Farrell	Rafferty
Callan	Geraghty	Kissane	Magennis	O'Flaherty	Riordan
Carroll	Gettings	Lafferty	Maguire	O'Gara	Ronan
Cassidy	Gleeson	Larkin	Maher	O'Flynn	Ryan
Clancy	Greene	Lewis	Marmion	O'Grady	Shaw
Cleary	Griffin	Long	Mangan	O'Hanlon	Shane
Clune	Gormley	Lynch	Marnane	O'Higgins	Sheehan
Collins	Hanly	MacClancy	Moloney	O'Keeffe	St John
Comerford	Hennessy	MacDermot	Mooney	O'Lalor	Sugrue
Connolly	Heery	MacGeoghegan	Moore	O'Leary	Tierney
Cormican	Heffernan	MacRaith	Muireagain	O'Loughlin	Tribes of
Crawford	Herlihy	McAnallen	Mullaney	O'Mahony	Galway
Cronin	Hickey	McAteer	Nolan	O'Malley	Troy
Crowe	Hogan	McAuliffe	Noonan	O'Meara	Turley
Crowley	Horgan	McCabe	O'Brien	O'Neill	Waldron
Cully	Hurley	McCarthy	O'Byrne	O'Rahilly	White
Curran	Hunt	McCullagh	O'Callaghan	O'Reilly	Whitty
Daly	Jones	McDonagh	O'Carragher	O'Rourke	Wingfield
Dalton	Joyce	McDuffee	O'Cathain	O'Shaughnessy	
Delaney	Kavanagh	McEgan	O'Connell	O'Scanlan	

LONGEST PEDIGREES

A thousand years ago, all the ruling families in Ireland claimed to be descended from Milesius. According to legend, Milesius, his sons and followers came to Ireland from Spain hundreds of years before the birth of Christ and conquered the earlier inhabitants of the country. The sons of Milesius divided Ireland between them. Their descendants ruled the country until they in turn were conquered by the Normans and the English.

It was important for Irish chiefs to be able to show that they were descended from Milesius, so they carefully preserved their pedigrees. When writing came to Ireland with the early Christians, pedigrees began to be written down. Some of these records were kept up to date as far as the middle of the seventeenth century.

The legend of Milesius is to be found in a twelfth-century Irish manuscript called 'The Book of Invasions'. The book gives Milesius's own pedigree, tracing him back first to Noah, then right back to Adam. Few people take it seriously today. Some other of the old Irish pedigrees are also inventions. If you were not related to Milesius and you were wealthy and powerful enough, you could get someone to forge a pedigree for you.

However, scholars accept that a lot of the information in old Irish manuscripts is true. Some Irish people can trace their ancestors back to the fifth century. The O'Neills of Ulster have the oldest documented pedigree in Western Europe, older than any European royal family.

REAL CLAN CHIEFS

Ancient Ireland was a patchwork of small independent kingdoms. The chief (rí) of a kingdom was elected by the sons, grandsons and great-grandsons of the previous chief. He had no special title, he was referred to by his surname. The chief of the O'Donnells, for example was simply called 'O'Donnell' or 'The O'Donnell'. Hugh O'Neill was the last great Irish chief. When he fled from Ulster in 1607, the old Irish system of government was at an end.

Many people have claimed to be descended from Irish chiefs. When Edward MacLysaght was put in charge of the Genealogical Office in 1943 he investigated those claims. He found some to be false or unprovable, but accepted sixteen as genuine. The work has continued since MacLysaght's time. Today, twenty Gaelic Chiefs are recognized.

President Robinson formally received the State-recognized Chiefs at Áras an Uachtaráin in October 1991.

The chiefs meet several times a year under the chairmanship of The Maguire of Fermanagh. Their organization is called the Standing Council of Irish Chiefs and Chieftains.

One thing that everyone wants to know when he/she sets about tracing the family tree is, how far am I likely to get back? In the case of most Irish people the answer is: not farther than 1800. Certainly, some people can do better, but it is also true to say, that some people cannot even get that far.

The Irish ancestors of John F. Kennedy and Ronald Reagan, both Presidents of the USA, and those of Paul Keating, Prime Minister of Australia, were no different to millions of other Irish people. The greatest family history experts in the world have researched the very ordinary Irish families of these men. In the case of all three, they failed to locate information on any ancestor born before 1800. This is only to be expected because almost all Irish records that were made before 1800 are about the wealthy landowners and not the ordinary people who rented farms and worked the land.

THE IRISH GENEALOGICAL CONGRESS

In countries where family history is a popular hobby, large conventions are held each year. People gather together to listen to lectures, to talk to experts, browse through bookstalls and generally learn more about the subject. The first convention of this kind to be held in Ireland took place over a seven-day period in September 1991. It was called the First Irish Genealogical Congress.

It was attended by 400 people. Most of them came from outside Ireland: Argentina, Australia, Canada, England, France, the Isle of Man, the Netherlands, New Zealand, Scotland and the USA.

Why were the Irish in the minority at their own Congress? For two reasons. Family history has not yet become a popular hobby in Ireland. Secondly, tens of millions of people who live outside Ireland have Irish ancestors and are anxious to find out more about them.

The organizers plan to hold a similar event every three years. You can find out more about the Congress by writing to the Genealogical Office, 2 Kildare Street, Dublin.

THE GENEALOGICAL OFFICE

The oldest office of state in Ireland that still functions is the Genealogical Office. It is first mentioned in history in 1482 during the reign of Richard II, though it was probably set up soon after the Norman invasion. One of its most important functions, which it still carries out today, is the granting and registering of coats of arms. Anybody who wishes to have his own personal coat of arms should write to the Chief Herald of Ireland at the Genealogical Office, 2 Kildare Street, Dublin 2. But be warned, it costs about £750.

The Genealogical Office runs a personal consultancy service throughout the year. For a fee of £20, you can go in and talk to an expert on family history for 30 to 45 minutes. Every year about 800 avail of this service, so it is wise to make an appointment before going along.

COAT OF ARMS

You can buy coats of arms for almost any surname. Most look impressive, especially those that are painted in bright colours and mounted on hardwood shields. Before you invest in one to hang in your hall or over your fireplace, remember that coats of arms belong to particular families, not to all those who share a common surname.

To be entitled to a coat of arms you must, at least, be able to prove that it was in use by your family for three generations or one hundred years. Ideally, you should be able to show unbroken male descent from a person to whom arms were granted and registered in the Genealogical Office.

Coats of arms are like titles. They were awarded at particular times to particular persons. Only the descendants of those persons have any right to use them. Your name may be Hugh O'Neill, but that does not make you Earl of Tyrone.

Still, there is another side to the story. Coats of arms are very attractive ornaments. People often display the crests of their favourite soccer club, without ever pretending to membership. You can take a certain pride in the fact that someone of your surname was awarded a coat of arms at some stage. Display it if you like.

If you read the second half of this book it should help you to get to know your ancestors a bit better. Their names and other details about them are in various collections of documents. You can learn about these collections and search them. Alternatively, you can pay a professional genealogist to do the searching, or you can get one of the county-based heritage centres to unearth some facts for you. Any of those ways should enable you to push your family tree back as far as about 1800 or perhaps further if you are lucky.

Even if you do no more research, you can still learn more about your ancestors simply by looking round you. Ireland as it is today was made by them. Everything from our ancient megalithic tombs to our attitude towards the police is a product of the people who lived in Ireland before us.

Whether we are aware of it or not, the things we do and feel and think are largely the result of our parents' influence. They in turn were influenced by their own parents and so on, back into history. This link with the past is sometimes called tradition. In a sense, it is how our ancestors whisper to us.